The Circles Of Life

The Circles Of Life

Mary E. Cole

iUniverse, Inc.
New York Lincoln Shanghai

The Circles Of Life

iUniverse books may be ordered through booksellers or by contacting:

iUniverse
2021 Pine Lake Road, Suite 100
Lincoln, NE 68512
www.iuniverse.com
1-800-Authors (1-800-288-4677)

Because of the dynamic nature of the Internet, any Web addresses or links contained in this book may have changed since publication and may no longer be valid.

The views expressed in this work are solely those of the author and do not necessarily reflect the views of the publisher, and the publisher hereby disclaims any responsibility for them.

ISBN: 978-0-595-47899-6

Printed in the United States of America

With love I give glory and thanks to the Heavenly Divine. I dedicate this book to all the great storytellers before me and for their contribution to history along the way. I give thanks to a community and the mentors that unified it. Above all, I give thanks to three incredible women, my mother, Mrs. Roberta Lane, my grandmother (deceased), Mrs. Josephine Howard, and last but not least, my mentor, Mrs. Ada Lee. Thanks to their motivation and encouragement, I have come this far by faith. To my family and friends with all my love, thank you.

Contents

1

Belief

All that you accomplish or fail to accomplish with your life is the direct results of your thoughts.

—*(James Allen)*

There comes a time in life if you live past fifty years of age and gain a little wisdom, you will realize you have come a full circle in life. You start out an infant, needing to be protected, fed, clothe, taught to speak, walk, read and all the needs that come with raising a child. As a teenager you have dreams, hopes, desire and energy with the motivation to make your mark in the world. Keep away from people who try to belittle your ambition. Some people always do that, but the really great ones make you feel that you too can become great. The easiest thing to find on earth is someone to tell you all the things you cannot do. Association brings on assimilation. Do the things you fear and the death of fear is certain.

One Friday, a fishing pal and I decided to travel from Atlanta to Pensacola, Florida to do some deep sea fishing. Once we reached the Florida line we ran into a hard rain storm. He was not the traveler I was and began to slow down to a crawl and decided to pull the car under one of the overpasses. I ask could I drive and he said yes. I hadn't driven three miles before we reached the sunshine. Behind was the storm, ahead was the sunshine. Sometime you have to believe if you push on you'll leave the storm behind. Many people work very hard to succeed and stop at the one yard line.

We are all the same in this one notion; the potential for greatness lives within each of us. As an adolescent we are mostly self absorb, which is normal. As an adult we realize the world is just not centered on one individual. All worthwhile goals come at a price and the coins with which we pay are concentration, persistence and desire.

Married with a small child I found myself on my way to basic training in the Army Reserve at the age of twenty seven. How was I bamboozled into signing up for the Army? It is called working with a recruiter; they never give up. Even my co-worker had signed up with the Air Force recruiter, but she was prior service so she did not go to basic, just drills. Some women came thinking they were going to a resort. Some could not endure even though they had committed themselves. A few would cry all through the night calling and begging their families to come and get them. But there were some even older than myself that was determined to succeed and they did.

Basic training was not a joke up at four a.m., formation, and then the four mile runs before breakfast. It doesn't take motivation and drive to be on the bottom, but you have to harness your will to be on the top. There is no education like adversity. If there is no enemy within, then the enemy outside cannot harm you. Stand up to crisis don't let yourself down. During basic we learned to function as one united. The hardest part of basic training for me was sleeping outside in tents enduring the rain without a bath for three days. Every little bug and creature you can think about wants to warm up in your tent. And I have issues with bugs. I made up my mind once I was hooked, lined and sink to give it my best shot and make the best of the weeks to come. Learn from my instructors instead of resisting them and I made it. How is it that many individuals, who possess only limited capabilities, manage to attract great admiration for extraordinary results?

Once we began to educate ourselves and chase careers, marry and have kids, dreams and priorities began to change. If you are one of those well discipline individuals that stayed on track, I truly commend you for a job well done. Some people put up with a lot of foolishness because they fear dieing and being alone, I believe in a one to a box theory. A mirror reflects a man or a woman face, but what he or she is really like is shown by the kind of friends they chooses.

Very often we are our own worst enemy as we foolishly build stumbling blocks on the path that leads to success and happiness, such as blaming others, having no goals and quitting too soon. Sometime many become derailed early in the game of life. After the storm come the rainbow if you look for it because, your thoughts can make you or break you. You can do what you are good at or you can do what you love, seek and live your dreams. Believe in yourself or nobody else will. I would rather try to succeed and fail than to try to do nothing and succeed. All that you accomplish or fail to accomplish with your life is the direct results of your thoughts.

In The Circles Of Life you make have to choose between the....

(The Chicken and the Eagle)

Once upon a time there was an eagle's nest that sat on top of the highest mountain peak. A strong wind came and blew an egg out of the nest and it rolled down the mountain into a valley and ended up in a chicken farm. The mother hen saw the little eagle egg and said "what a funny looking chicken egg, but I will sit on it and make it my little chicken." The mother hen sat on the egg until it hatched.

When it hatched, out came this big beak, big feet and huge wings. The mother looked at the little bird and said. "What a funny looking chicken but you can be one of my little chickens." And even though the bird was born with eagle genes and eagle chromosomes, it was born in chicken surroundings. So it thought it was a chicken, it walked like a chicken and it talked like a chicken. It thought like a chicken and even began to dream like a chicken. It biggest dream was to get on top of the fence and crow like a rooster. It figured if it could only do that then the other birds would not laugh and make fun of the fact that it looked different. But each time it dreamed that dream, it would say to itself, you know you can never get on top of that fence! You know they always told you chickens can't fly! So it didn't even try. It would just give up and walk away.

One day while standing out in the barnyard it looked up and saw the most magnificent sight it had ever seen. It saw the sight of an eagle flying majestically across the sky, like the king of the sky. The little bird was so amazed that it shouted with all that was within, "What are you? What are you? The big eagle with it powerful hearing and powerful eyesight saw the little bird and flew straight down and said, "What am I? What are you?" and the little bird said; I am a chicken. The big eagle looked the little bird straight in the eyes and said, look at my face, you look just like me, look at my beak, you look just like me, look at my wings, you look just like me, friend you are not a chicken, you are an eagle! Flap your wings and fly like the eagle you were born to be. The little bird flapped its wings and he flew; he soared above the clouds.

Make your mark: Some of us were born to soar like eagles but due to our surrounding continue to peck on the ground like chickens. Friends are like elevators they can take you up or they can bring you down. I hear, I forget, I see, I remember, I do I understand.

2

Cruelty

o o o o o o o o o o o o o o o o o o o o o o o o o o o o o o o o o o

When you become caught up in the heady pursuit of success you always run the risk of losing far more than you gain unless you are careful.

—(Dr, Allen Fromme)

Today is Thursday and I am sitting in the den area attached to a master bathroom, I am with one of my clients I can hear her talking about her past experiences long ago as though they were yesterday. I am a retired accountant, free lancing as a motivational storyteller and caregiver and my client is full of life and energy wanting to enjoy and soak up what ever time is left.

The love of money can and do change some people. Family disagreements can mushroom sometime out of proportion and cause a rift in the bonds of families. Her sister now had plenty of money and bad health. Without good health and the love of your family, what good is wealth?

I began to think the night before about all the opportunities I had to direct my life in a different direction and make different choices but here I am. I have always enjoyed the companionship of the elderly since I was a teenager. Maybe they had more patience and wisdom and willing to take the time to listen. I had dreams of travel, adventure and a desire to help motivate others.

My love of the elderly bought me in contact with my first experience of meeting a wolf in sheep clothing, better known as a chameleon able to change colors due to its surroundings. I met this young man a nephew of one of the elderly and my life became derailed. He was mush older and thought to be more mature. He could charm honey from bees but behind closed doors the worst kind of evil hid within, a jealous hearted, controlling, and a vengeful spirit, the kind that smile and beat the life out of you. Your temper is like a fire, it gets very destructive

4

when it gets out of control. A person's true character is revealed by what he does when no one is watching and critical spirit is like poison ivy, it only takes a little contact to spread its venom.

Today in the media two well known and prosperous preachers are in the news for domestic violence Mr. and Mrs. Weeks. Early in the morning they are fighting in a hotel parking lot. He kicked, stumped and beat her down. A man is never in worse company than when he flies into a rage and is beside himself. I have learned you can't judge the book by looking at the cover it is best to open it and read it. There are lots of little boys in men bodies and there are lots of little girls in women bodies but sometime you don't realize what you have until they throw a tantrum geared toward you and all hell breaks loose. A soft answer turns away wrath, but harsh words can cause quarrels and gentle words causes' life and health. The individual must control the deepest perception of him, least he be overwhelmed by the forces of negative thoughts and defeat in those around him. The basic motive for success is the driving force of envy and jealousy. In the mist of change there are no bargains and guarantees, a price must always be paid in advance, and in full. The man or woman who sets a trap for others will get caught in it themselves. Roll a boulder down on someone, and it will roll back and crush you.

A dear friend of mine in the military; husband was very mild and meek; she had never seen him angry. One day she decided she had to see was he normal and went to work to make him mad it took a lot but when she woke up she had broken ribs and he did not remember a thing it was as if he left his body. I know because I've been there. There is a difference between a man and woman that is mad than a mad man and mad woman.

Most people that are slow to anger are very dangerous and pushed too far will literally snap. Speak when you are angry and you will make the best speech you will ever regret. When you become caught up in the heavy pursuit of success you always run the risk of loosing far more than you gain unless you are careful.

In The Circles Of Life many are….

(Losing In Las Vegas)

Steve had a dream. He wanted to spend two magical weeks in Las Vegas. He had saved enough money to be able to gamble and not worry about the loss. He had enough to see all the new shows, eat well, and stay in the very best hotel. Steve checked in and put on his best clothes. He looked sharp. Downstairs, shooting craps, he got lucky immediately. The management began sending him free drinks, people gathered to watch.

Across the table, Steve noticed a gorgeous redhead. This is the one, he thought, but how to meet her? What line do I use? Don't I know you from somewhere before? Didn't you go to my high school? What is your sign? Then he remembered reading somewhere that women like honesty best of all. Steve approached the redhead. "I don't usually do this," he said" but you look so interesting, do you mind if I talk to you? Buy you a drink?" The woman smiled, her eyes lit up as he talked to her. Steve realized they had a lot in common, they both loved the outdoors. They both divorced and had no children. They each loved horses and dogs but hated broccoli. Let's go get dinner, he suggested. "Oh Steve," she said, "you are on such a wonderful roll. I hate to see you stop. Let me be your lady luck." He won five hundred dollars, then a thousand, two thousand, three thousand. "That's enough," said Steve, "we can buy the finest meal in town with this."

The conversation over dinner was relaxed and interesting Steve felt as if he'd known this woman all his life. After dinner, she said, "Why don't you come up to my hotel room? Just what he'd been hoping for. Once they were in her room, she began mixing drinks. "Steve, have you ever had a white zombie?" she asked. "No," he replied," but I'm willing to try anything. She mixed the drinks and he drank his in one gulp.

The next thing Steve knew he was waking up in a strange hotel room. The woman was gone; he had a terrible pain in his back. He saw a needle run from his arm to an IV stand. He couldn't understand what had happen to him. Steve reached over, picked up the phone and dialed 911. He told the operator he was in a strange hotel room and he had an IV running from his arm. "Sir," she said, "slowly reach behind you and see do you have a bandage on your back." Steve reached behind him. Sure enough, it was there right above his hip. He said, "yes, it is a gauze bandage, a big one and my back hurts like crazy." Well sir, said the emergency operator, I'm afraid someone has stolen yours kidney, you see there's a syndicate here in Las Vegas that's stealing kidneys and selling them overseas. You've been caught in a very clever and vicious scan.

Make your mark: Many of us are looking for love in all the wrong places. One night of pleasure, can cause you a lifetime of pain. You can't change how you are going to die but you can change how you are going to live.

3

Education

o o o o o o o o o o o o o o o o o o o o o o o o o o o o o o o o o o
He who asks a question is a fool for five minuets; he who does
not ask a question is a fool forever. We are all born ignorant, but
to stay ignorant is a choice, without some form of education you
are lost.

—*(Chinese Proverb)*

Sweet Sadie a song about a real grandmother, the kind that played a strong part
in the rearing of their grandchildren and they were valued. I grew up in a small
town. You can say a community helped to raise me. There were plenty of food
and someone, a grandmother, aunt or cousin always at home. There were mentors someone who cared about the children and their well being. The best inher-
itance parents can leave their children is a good example. If you give a man a fish
you feed him for a day, if you teach a man to fish, you feed him for a lifetime.

The mentors made sure we got to church and had a recreation center for our
outlet. I grew up with aunts and cousins my own age, so we explored the woods,
fruit farms, ditches and graveyards as kids do it taught me courage. Many good
people have failed, because they had the wishbone where the backbone should
have been. There are two lasting bequests we can give our children, one our roots
and the other our wings.

Growing up in this environment grounded me and gave me family values. It is
funny when you are in a small town you desire the life of the big city. The world
and people will educate you if you are receptive and listen. I decided to leave for
Miami after my experience with the chameleon, flight or continue to fight. Out
of sight out of mind I say, people will always find other victims.

Recently I worked with battered and abused women and my experience happened so long ago I forgot it. The best way to get even is to forget. I chose to fight

back and make a change for awhile. I don't understand why some women persist on the abuse and choose to continue to live in the range of the abuser. If you can get the heck out of town for a while and still there are no guarantees. Unfortunately, that is one of the prices of life, no guarantees, but nothing beat a failure, but a try. The gift to us is life, what we do with it is our gift to life. Although I realize some don't have the strength and courage to battle some demons but once a mind is stretched by a new idea, will never regain its original dimension. Knowledge is power.

I've always loved bright lights and tall buildings but it was really tough being young with just a high school education to reach for the moon, I was lucky to reach a moon pie. If you don't stand for something you will fall for anything. It is better to be silent and be considered a fool than to speak and remove all doubt. I learned to listen. The purpose of learning is growth and our minds unlike our bodies, can continue growing as we continue to live.

Attending college at home was not an option for me I was ready to leave and see other places. Parents can advise you about life but some success and mistakes you have to make on your own to grow. Even though their advice could save you wasted time and money. One must follow their own dreams and some dreams take you full circle, right back where you started from.

Relocation was different and challenging but a beautiful experience. People are virtually the same wherever you go. Some may look, speak, and act differently but in the mix of it all they are about family and friends. It is easy to move but hard to stay. He who asks a question is a fool for five minutes; he who does not ask a question is a fool forever. We are all born ignorant, but to stay ignorant is a choice, without some form of education you are lost.

In The Circles Of Life you will meet the....

(The Handsome Man)

There was this man, a very good looking and handsome but he wasn't very smart. When he was young everyone told him how good he looked he was the most beautiful child. As a teenager he was even more handsome. One day he told his parents he was going to quit school if he could work on his body he could be successful, against their advice he did. He went to the gym each day and his body looked great but wasn't winning the body builders competition.

One day while leaving the gym he met this incredible beautiful woman and they began to date and soon fell in love. It wasn't long before they were married. His parents helped them to establish their own place as a wedding gift. He still continued to go to the gym each day until one day his wife noticed they were getting bills that was not being paid and he needed a job.

Now he always dreamed of joining the police academy. In order to join you had to apply and pass an entrance exam. Somehow he managed to apply and they were obligated to test him. So they decided to first give him an oral exam. The examiner escorted him to a room and began to ask him questions. His first question was what is two plus two? The man thought for a while held up two fingers and said eleven. The examiner said, you are truly amazing and the man just smiled. The examiner asks the second question, what two days of the week start with T? The man thought for awhile and said, today and tomorrow, the examiner looked at the man and said, you are truly amazing and the man just smiled. The third question the examiner asks who was Abraham Lincoln. The man thought and thought and finally said, I don't know but I can found out for you. The examiner looked at the man and said, you are truly amazing and the man just smiled. So the examiner said O.K. you go out and found out who was Abraham Lincoln and you let us know. The man got really excited and returned home. His wife met him at the door and ask him did he get the job, he said yes, of course, they thought I was truly amazing. She said, really; He said sure, they already have me on a Top Secret Mission to found out who is Abraham Lincoln.

Make your mark: Sometime things are not what they seem. The choices you make, determines the future you create. The mind is a terrible thing to waste.

4

Faith

o o o o o o o o o o o o o o o o o o o o o o o o o o o o o o o o o o

Fear knocked at the door. Faith opened it. And lo, there was no
one there. Do the things you fear and the death of fear is certain.

—*(Emerson)*

Before leaving for Miami I was examined, and tested for the Air Force but did
not take the oath because I had to wait for the slot I qualified for, they were very
selective. During this time I had moved and when they called it was mid summer
and I had lost interest one of the problems of being young, a short attention span.
It wasn't long before I returned home and went to technical school to learn a
trade. I was fortunate to be hired by the Federal government it gave me a decent
income and stability. Today what is now common, to fall in love, live together,
have a baby, and marry was not common then. Isn't it funny how times have
changed? I met a soldier, fell in love, married and had a beautiful daughter. The
only problem was he had a hidden gambling problem, I say it was hidden sometimes we only see what we want to see after the fact. The wealth from gambling
quickly disappears, wealth from hard work grows.

The road to success is always under construction. You will encounter potholes,
detours and delays, but you must keep your eye on the goal and keep moving forward. Derailed once more I became a single parent trying to get out of a deep
hole. Never underestimate the power of dreams and the influence of the human
spirit. Life is too short to be small. We must all suffer one or two things the pain
of self discipline or the pain of regret and disappointment. Sometime we become
afraid after adversities, fear of change, fear of rejection, and even fear of success.
You would be surprised at the people that actually sabotage their lives when they
start becoming more and more successful. Don't judge those who try and fail
judge only those who fail to try.

Henry David Thoreau wrote: I know of no more encourage fact than the unquestionable ability of a man or woman to elevate his or her life by conscious endeavor; be a model of victory instead a victim of circumstance. If you don't have time to do it right, when you are going to have time to do it again. If you fail, land on your back because if you can look up you can get up. My mentor proved miracles do happen. She was ill and been in bed for years. Today in her eighties she is driving, attending church and enjoying life. Faith can change illness to health.

We are all the same in this notion; the potential for greatness lives within each of us. Perhaps the biggest break anyone could ever receive is to decide exactly what it is he or she wants and then become obsessed with obtaining it. I often think of our childhood days of playing in the cemetery and playing in the ditch. Good timber does not grow with ease; the stronger the wind, the stronger the trees. Sometime it was a challenge to get out of the ditch. We would have to travel until we found a suitable spot to crawl out of the hole. One day while we were exploring in this deep hole I felt something on my shoulders. I looked and there were two big eyes with funny feet looking at me, it was a praying mantis, a bug and off I went running, no one could catch me, I was screaming and no one could keep me in that ditch, like a flash of lighting, I was gone.

It is far better to aim too high and fall short, than it is to aim too low and hit right on the mark. People may doubt what you say but they always believe what you do. All things are possible to him that believes. Fear knocked on the door. Faith opened it. And lo there was no one there. Face the thing you fear and the death of fear is certain.

In The Circles Of Life you will one day visit the....

(The Cemetery)

There was once this man and he worked until midnight every night and occasionally he would walk home though the cemetery. This particular night while walking home through the cemetery the moon began to wane and even though it was absolutely dark he felt he could walk through the cemetery safely. While walking though the cemetery the man feet all of a sudden slipped from under him and he found himself falling in a newly dug grave. The man tried desperately to get out of the hole but the more he struggled the deeper he seemed to get because the man was too short and the hole was too deep. So the man decided he would just wait for the grave diggers to come in the morning and they could lift him out of the hole. He decided he would go in the corner pull his jacket over his head and get him some sleep.

One hour later another wondering citizen came walking through the cemetery and all of a sudden his feet slipped from under him and he found himself falling in the grave on the other side. He tried desperately to get out of the hole but the man was too short and the grave was too deep. The more he tried the more dirt seems to fall upon him. The man tried everything he could think of to get out of the hole. So he stood there contemplating what to do next. Over in the corner the man is watching the man trying to get out of the hole, so he decided to speak. He stood up, removed his coat from over his head, walked over to the man and said, "boy you ain"t never getting out of this hole that way, all of a sudden the man was gone, out of the hole and out of the cemetery in a flash. They both had the ability to get out of the hole but needed a little motivation.

Make your mark: When you found yourself in a tight place and everything seems to go against you, until you feel like you can't hold on one minuet longer, never give up then because that is the time and the place the tides will turn. Remember quitters never win and winners never quit.

5

Blessings

There is a song call Papa was a Rolling stone where ever he laid his hat was his home. My father was a farmer and he was good at planting seeds in fertile gardens but he just never remembered to come back and water them. You could say he was like Johnny Apple Seed but nature watered, fed, and protected the seeds. He only believed in the harvest. A garden without water is like a baby without milk, it can't survive. Some goes through life believing only in the harvest never thinking of the labor. You cannot continue to receive and never give. It is against the law of averages. Many only think what about me? Even though they know they are bless but refuse to be a blessing. Forget yourself for others and others will not forget you. You must water the garden sometime. Time is more valuable than money because time is irreplaceable.

A song called, "We will have a good time then," is a message a father is giving to his son. He always brings him gifts and says we will have a good time then son. Even when he brought him a foot ball he didn't have time to play with him, not now son but we will have a good time then. The boy would always say I just want to be like you dad, I just want to be like you. One day the man is old and the son is in college and the man wants the son to spend some time with him and the son say's not now dad but we will have a good time then dad, we will have a good time then. You can't undo the past, just fix the present.

The journey of a thousand miles began with a single step. My mother had me at a young age, her journey started then, to help me to become an adult. Having a child makes you a mother, raising a child makes you a woman. The measure of a one's character is not what he or she gets from their ancestors, but what he or she leaves their descendents. The bridge you burn now may be the one you later have to cross.

The secret of contentment is the realization that life is a gift not a right. My mother had to grow up quickly; with the help of her family and my stepfather they provided my needs. One of my parents biggest challenges were raising five girls. Children are gifts that can enhance your life especially in your old age. We all if we keep living return to the necessary basic, needing the love and protection of your love ones and friends. Many people today are living very long lives.

There are men and women participating in clubs or groups that cater to the ones that are a hundred years or older. Man's life expectancy is seventy eight years of age. It is great just to be able to share it with someone. Most children are not perfect but my two girls now adults and living on their own made my life an adventure. I don't know who loved zoos, parks, and having fun more. Caring for them made me more courageous, strong and focused.

You can choose your friends but you can't choose your family. Some people give very little but expect a lot. In order to plan your future wisely, it is necessary that you understand and appreciate your past. Many today are preparing in life moving forward and some are repairing life looking backward.

Feeling sorry for yourself, and your present condition, is not only a waste of energy but the worst habit you could possibly have. I had the blues because I had no shoes, until upon the street; I met a man who had no feet. Count your blessings and not your troubles. A man or woman wrapped in him or herself make a very small package. The dimensions of their lives become dwarfed and limited.

In The Circles Of Life you will have …

(Regrets)

A young man was getting ready to graduate from college. For many months he had admired a beautiful sports car in a dealer's showroom and knowing his father could well afford it, he told him that was all he wanted. As graduation day approached, the young man awaited signs that his father had purchased the car. Finally, on the morning of his graduation, his father called him into his private study. His father told him how proud he was to have such a fine son, and told him how much he loved him. He handed his son a beautifully wrapped gift box. Curious and somewhat disappointed, the young man opened the box and found a lovely leather-bound bible with the young man's name embossed in gold. Angry, he raised his voice to his father and said "With all your money, you give me a bible and stormed out of the house.

Many years passed and the young man was very successful in business. He had a beautiful home and wonderful family but realized his father was very old and thought perhaps he should go to him. He had not seen him since graduation day. Before he could make arrangements, he received a telegram telling him his father had passed away and willed all of his possessions to his son. He needed to come home immediately and take care of things.

When he arrived at his father's house, sudden sadness and regret filled his heart. He began to search through his father's important papers and saw the still gift-wrapped bible, just as he had left it years ago. With tears, he opened the bible and began to turn the pages. His father had carefully underlined a verse, Matt 7:11 "If you then who is evil know how to give good gifts to your children, how much more will your father who is in heaven give good things to those who ask him." As he read those words, a car key dropped from the back of the bible. It had a tag with the dealer's name, the same dealer who had the sport car he had desired. On the tag was the date of his graduation and the words PAID IN FULL.

Make your mark: How often we miss our blessings because we can't see pass our own desires. The saddest words of the tongue and pen, is to hear someone say, what might have been.

6

Uniqueness

○ ○
We are all born unique but most of us die a carbon copy. "To thine own self be true.

—(Shakespeare)

One night I was sitting outside on the deck, reflecting back on my life and thinking about the pioneers that had gone before me and the difference and impact they made on people lives. What did they have that was so unique? Some of them changed history. The one thing they did was to leave a paragraph or their name in a history book. Years from now when you are long gone only your legacy will be remembered. The poorest of all men is not the man without a cent but the man without a dream. Even a woodpecker owes his success to the fact that he uses his head. He who buries his talent is making a graved mistake. Even if you are famous now the people that know you will pass away as well as you and if there is nothing written about you it will all be forgotten. Ultimately, we are remembered for what we give, not for what we take.

It is about 9 a.m. I am with a client, she is a lovely old lady that has contributed a lot to humanity and can talk for hours none stop. At this time I am just sitting waiting on her to dress and take her shopping and for a ride to keep in contact with city changes. She has a lot of history behind her but who will know of her contributions. Man alone is the architect of his destiny. That is why I've decided storytelling is my calling in life and I must share it or write it or somehow leave a paragraph to be remembered. Maybe someday someone will know I was here on earth and tried to make a difference.

Les Brown once said, don't go where the path may lead you but go where there is no path and leave a trail. There are many small people doing big things. Once I lived in a city called, Union City, there I met a lady a divorcee raising two kids a boy and a girl. The little girl and my daughter were the same age, I got to know her and she was born with only one arm. Even though this was considered a handicap you would not know it. She combed their hair, cooked, did laundry, drove a car, washed clothes, played games, she could even sew and I thought she was amazing. Even during high school our cashier was born with no arms. She could count money and give change with her toes. I even heard she could type with her feet. I was mesmerized how she could move us alone in the lunch line as she received our money and tokens.

Many have unique talents they don't use. I too am accountable for my life and its contribution to humanity. Unless we leave something in history written or done something very unique it will not be passed alone. There are many talented, unique and great people the world will never know existed because they failed to show up or speak up. We are all born unique but most of us die a carbon copy. "To thine own self be true.

In The Circles Of Life you will see …

(The Rare Bird)

This man was at a restaurant when he heard two women talking about this unique, one of a kind rare bird that could speak five different languages; he decided to go on a worthwhile search looking for it. He was the sort that loved to keep and collect anything rare. The next morning he called some pet shops but no one had heard of the unique, one of a kind bird that could speak five different languages.

The man decided to go on a worldwide search for the bird and after an exhausting search, he then stopped in a small town to take care of some business and while observing the different shops he noticed a small pet shop across the street and decided to take a look and asks for more information and it was there he found the rare bird. He told the owner he had to go on a short trip and could he send the bird to his home in two days. When he arrived home in two days all excited he asked his wife had the bird arrived and she said yes, he said well where it is? She said it was in the oven, he said what? In the oven, that was one of a kind unique and rare bird that could speak five different languages. The wife said, well, why didn't it speak up?

Make your mark: The prizes in life we fail to win because we doubt the power within. Ones doubts are traitors and make us lose the good we would win by fearing to attempt.

7

Construction

"I will not permit any man to narrow and degrade my soul by making me hate him.

—*(Booker T. Washington)*

When you are young and chasing a career you never think of the obstacles you will face to earn a living. Some people succeed because they are destined to, but most people succeed because they are determined. It is not enough to qualify for the job but to have to go through the games people play. In life success can do one or two things; help you to grow up or help you to blow up. Two things that are hard on the heart, running upstairs and running down people. People who whittle you down are only trying to reduce you to their size.

Unfortunately, titles, income and material wealth can change even the most humble person if they are not grounded. The difference between ordinary and extraordinary is that little extra. When tyrants are placed in leadership positions they can make an average person a life of hell. As a federal worker there is something called an appraisal, this determines whether you qualify for a promotion or cash award and other incentives. Sometimes you have what they call clicks; they run in packs because alone they are ineffective. A good leader can enhance people lives and poor leadership can derailed people lives. Some leaders do not earn respect but demand it because on paper they have the title. In many cases they knew someone, slept with someone, blackmailed someone and down right lied on their application. About twenty percent of them really qualify.

The Air Force was downsizing and some workers found themselves doing jobs out of their field. I was assigned a gentleman that definitely was not office bound. But we made the best of the situation. He did his best and I picked up the pieces. He had a big heart and a great spirit and he gave it all he had. Eventually he was reassigned to the job he was qualified for and enjoyed doing. Anyway this click which consisted of three ladies all added together did not have the I.Q of a question mark. Decided they would deny me of a promotion or cash award by downgrading my performance. Once I reviewed the appraisal I refused to sign it. They decided to sign it for me. I took the case to the union and guess who was president of the union, the co-worker I had train. I had all kind of documentation of all of my work performance. Be careful how you treat people that same person may have to come to yours rescue one day. I got my award and was asked to keep hush, hush, about it. When someone ask you to keep secrets ask yourself why?

It is easy to work in the construction business tearing others down while building yourself up. Some even go around accusing others of making them the victim when in fact they are the culprit. Their choices are what cause the derailment in their lives. Failure in people is caused more by lack of determination than lack of talent. If you want to keep on getting what you are getting just keep on doing what you are doing. What you reap is what you sow.

A man or woman wrapped in themselves, makes a very small package. Someday you are going to need someone just keep living. I was taking a shower this morning and as I oiled myself down I realized all the energy it took to complete my task and how winded I was. Can you imagine at ninety-eight years of age how awful it would be without needed assistance? To think in life you don't need anyone is beyond me. It is said misery loves company. I will not permit any man to narrow and degrade my soul by making me hate him.

In The Circles Of Life you may be invited to….

(The CEO Party)

A CEO and member of Forbes 500 throwing a party, takes his executive on a tour of his opulent mansion. In the back of the property, the CEO has the largest swimming pool any of them has ever seen. The huge pool, however, is filled with hungry alligators.

The CEO says to his executives "I think an executive should be measured by courage. Courage is what made me CEO. So this is my challenge to each of you: If anyone has enough courage to dive into the pool, swim through those alligators, and make it to the other side, I will give that person anything they desire. My job, my money, my house, anything!" Everyone laughs at the outrageous offer and proceeds to follow the CEO on the tour of the estate.

Suddenly, they hear a loud splash. Everyone turns and sees the CFO, (Chief Financial Officer) in the pool, swimming for his life. He dodges the alligators left and right and makes it to the edge of the pool with his shoes. The flabbergasted CEO approaches the CFO and says; you are amazing. I've never seen anything like it in my life. You are brave beyond measure and anything I own is yours. Tell me what I can do for you." The CFO, panting for breath, looks up and says," "You can tell me who in the hell pushed me in the pool!"

Make your mark; In a leadership position be careful how you treat people because some will pull you out of danger and some will push you into danger.

8

Laziness

o o o o o o o o o o o o o o o o o o o o o o o o o o o o o o o o o o o o o
Among the greatest of human tragedies are the wasted lives of
those who fail, after enjoying success lose their desire to ever try
again.

—*(Frederick Van Rensselaer Day)*

I lived in the city of Atlanta for many years as a single mom and it was a challenge
and a delight. The girls and I enjoyed the many activities the city had to offer, the
zoo, park, fishing, boating, movies and most of all Six Flags Amusement Park.
Although I was a single mom I always made quality time for the girls. It is not
how much time you spend with your family it is the quality of time you spend. I
worked a full time job as I served in the Army Reserve as a weekend warrior. I
always maintained a part time business for backup this helped our finances. Good
and faithful friends also played an important roll in my life.

Someone once said, if you have just five real friends in your lifetime you are
rich. A man or woman with friends is never a failure. I truly believe my true
friends made an emotional, physical and financial difference in my life. We
shared our social and spiritual lives together, some were married and some were
single parents also. During this time I was in a long term intimate relationship for
many years. The relationship was off and on due to unwanted baggage. You can
change a persons environment but you can't change their mind, they can hear the
truth and still reject it.

When you don't have a since of value it is easy to become victimized. My
friend had for over thirty years carried the misery of a broken relationship and
family disappointments in every relationship he was involved in. Sorrow look
back, worry looks around, faith looks up. Why do some people make innocent

victims pay the price for some one's else mistakes? You should never let adversity get you down except on your knees.

I met a wonderful older lady that became ill. She became ill and was placed in a facility. In less than one month her daughter had a yard sale of her belonging and what she didn't sale she left wasting beside the road. She hasn't seen very much her daughter since. Some people are ungrateful even if you love and be good to them but you can't be bitter. After years of trying I could never get this person to move on and enjoy life he did not know how to. He suspected every one of evil deeds; many people live and talk in their past. Low self esteem, fear, jealousy, alcohol and laziness was so dominate in his life you could not tear down this wall because he refused to change and continued to be imprisoned in his mind. Fear seized him.

Life can only be understood by looking backward, but it must be lived by looking forward. Sometimes we are so busy adding up trouble we forget to count our blessings. He had a wonderful life and wonderful family but he was stuck and couldn't move on blinded by his past. We were stuck in neutral and one of us had to drive. Good relationships are ruined because one individual cannot let go of past hurts, disappointments and unfulfilled dreams as a child.

We all get hurt and sometime and life does not always go as we planned but when the going get tough the tough get going. If you continue to bath in your misery, the past, you will get left behind. Some people are left behind and the rapture hasn't even happened yet. When you don't learn to master your emotions, your emotions will master you. You cannot move uphill thinking downhill thoughts. Many become so overwhelmed by their past they don't live in the present, they just exist. I was asked by a friend why some people don't care about anything even their basic needs. They will not work expecting a handout for all their needs. Among the greatest of human tragedies are the wasted lives of those who fail, after enjoying success lose their desire to ever try again.

In The Circles Of Life you will one day meet....

(The Cowbird)

Too lazy and shiftless to build her own nest and rear her own young, the cowbird a parasite blackbird may sometimes be seen sneaking through the trees and bushes in search of some nest left unguarded for a moment. In such a nest she will slyly lay her egg and then slip off, leaving the cares of incubation and motherhood to the foster parents.

The bird is an acknowledged parasite and depraved with no friends among man or bird. However villain and delinquent as it is it is an interesting bird. The bird gets it name from its habit of frequenting pastures where cattle are grazing, where large flocks feed on the insects stirred up by the cows as they graze. So close the birds keep right under the feet of the cattle you wonder how they avoid being stepped upon. The depraved bird breeds in the Atlantic coast states this bird imposes upon over ninety-two species of birds. The most frequent victims are the warblers, vireos and the song and the chipping sparrows.

The Cowbird is usually careful to choose a nest of a species smaller than her, so that her egg being larger than those that rightfully belong in the nest, get more warmth and hatches sooner. The young cowbird grows rapidly and is vociferous in its demands for food. This result in the rightful nestlings often being smothered crowded out of the nest or starved. This havoc and destruction are devastating in other bird families by these parasite birds. The Cowbird has even been seen removing an egg from the Red-eyed Vireo nest and dropped her own in its place. And yet the young strangling, reared by foster parents, usually at the cost of the lives of their own young, is an ingrate. As soon as fully reared it deserts these parents and joins flocks of its own outlaw kind.

Make your mark: Man alone of all creatures of earth can change his own pattern by changing the inner attitude of their minds; can change the outer aspects of their lives.

9

Change

Who you are speaks so loudly I can't hear what you are saying.

—(Ralph Waldo Emerson)

You can lead a horse to water but you can't make him drink, you send a child to school but you can't make them think. Some people refuse to think they need to change but want others to continue to accommodate there bad choices. The only fool bigger than the person who knows it all is the person who argues with him. Too many people spend money they haven't earned, to buy things they don't want, to impress people they don't like. Man cannot discover new oceans unless he has the courage to lose sight of the shore.

I received a call from a male friend I haven't heard from in a long time. The conversation was about many of his friends that made bad choices in life and because he is an entrepreneur they look for him for moral and financial support. The problem is that so many now need his support he can't continue. Falling down doesn't make you a failure, but staying down does.

One particular friend I knew well had all the advantages life could offer, a nice home, car, career and loving companionship but, (SOS) he called this stuck on stupid. It never occurred to me because it seems so degrading to refer to someone this way but once I thought about this he was right. There are many people making the same mistakes over and over again because they are stuck in a time warp, never growing and refusing to make changes.

So often you hear people with pride say, I am still the same person I was thirty years ago haven't anything about me changed. Sometime they don't have to tell you because you can see it for yourself. Unfortunately, I can't say that, my energy level changed and some other things did too but people seldom think before they speak and don't realize the impact of what they are saying. Words can enhance your life and words can destroy your life. I too have watched this same friend life that is stuck become derailed because she refused to change or grow but she had the incredible ability to always tell and advise people on how to live there lives.

Some people can give good advice but not take it. The train of failure usually turns on the track of laziness. She lost a long term marriage, home, friends and career because it was her way or no way. This can cause relationships to grow apart and eventually one may hit the highway. Everything comes with a price are you ready to pay what it takes? Who you are speaks so loudly I can't hear what you are saying.

In The Circles Of Life some will be left behind because they will....

(Not Fly South This Winter)

A little robin named Sport decided he'd rather not fly south for the winter. He refused to make a change he was staying right where he was no matter what. As snow began to fall and streams iced over, he reluctantly came to the conclusion that he'd made a big mistake and he'd better head south. As Sport rose high into the scurry sky, the air felt even colder and the winds more fierce. He flew as straight south as he could and yet the wind threw him about with utter disdain.

After flying for what seems like forever, his wings began to ice over. Fly as he might, his wings soon froze to the point of almost no movement and so he half glided half plummeted toward earth. Through frosted eyebrows he saw an open spot among the trees. Navigating as best he could, Sport plummeted into a farmyard and landed among the cows. He rolled over twice, skidded into a clump of hay and just lay there regretting the day he decided to spend the winter in Maine.

At this very moment and with total unawareness of the robin, one of the cows came along and dropped a warm wet cow pie right on top of him. Struggling frantically, Sport managed to stick his head up and take a breath. He gasped at the smell, but immediately noticed that whatever he was in, it was very warm. He soon stopped shivering. As he became warm and comfortable, he did as birds do, he began to chirp. Closing his eyes Sport thought thoughts of the southern sun. Spontaneously, he chirped again. Unfortunately for Sport, his chirping sparked the curiosity of Freddy, the barnyard cat. So Freddy, who did as cats do, came along to investigate. He found Sport, chirping away with his eyes closed. Since Sport had no idea what was going on around him he was an easy target for Freddy. Freddy hauled Sport out of the manure pile and then promptly ate him.

Make your mark: Not everyone who dumps on you is your enemy. Not everyone who hauls you out of manure is your friend and above all, if you are warm and comfortable, keep your eyes open and your mouth shut.

10

Habits

"An idle mind is the devil's workshop. Man is happier who lives on his own labor.

—*(The Englishman)*

Success is a journey, not a destination. In life sometime things do not go as planned.

Many times dreams are shattered so bad, some just give up on life completely. My cousin had a promising football career in college. One major injury changed his world from one of success to drugs and defeat. His thought of only football.

The mind is like a garden it doesn't care what you plant but it will return to you what you plant. If you think failure and defeat that is exactly what it will go to work to do. If you think success and victory it can produce that to but you can't plant night shed a deadly poison plant and expect a juicy red sweet apple in return. This is against the law of nature. The mind controls the body the body does not control the mind.

Often I think of the movie, Cool Hand Luke with Steve McQueen. Steve spent most of his years in prison for petty crimes. His greatest achievement in life was breaking the record in prison for eating the most boiled eggs. He was guilty of a wasted life. Can you imagine living a lifetime fifty or sixty years and this is your legacy but at least he had a legacy to leave and follow. If you reach for higher goals the mind will take you up, if you reach for lower goals it will take you down.

I knew a beautiful young woman that could have been a top model. She was educated, tall and had a great body but wanted to get rich quick. She worked as a school teacher for a short while and decided she would become a foster mother because the pay was good and less students. The responsibility of caring for trouble children never occurred to her. Against the advice of family and friends because she was young, single with no children of her own cautioned her of the problems she could face. Even with this information she refused to listen because the money would be great. The first step to wisdom is silence, the second is listening. She quit teaching and the agency placed her with foster kids. One kid in particular has issues, he had been mentally and physically abused and he was angry. One day while he was having a tantrum he almost fell and she reached to grab him and dislocated his shoulder. With child abuse being so ramped she was made an example. Regardless of all the good she had done and many references from co-workers and friends who testified in her behalf she was sent to prison. The greed made her a victim of circumstances.

Free lunch seminars with no strings attached, I am constantly getting these invitations. But free lunch seminars are feeding you for one purpose to get you to buy something maybe not at the meeting but eventually. Federal and state securities regulators said they found everything misleading or exaggerated claims to outright fraud. The man or woman who wants to do right will get a rich reward but the man or woman that want to get rich quick will quickly fail. The glory of a young man or woman is their strength: The glory of an old man and woman is their experience. So there is no free lunch.

Many people are looking for the easy road in life; some even want something for nothing, there is always a price to pay. Now if we have to pay to die and be buried, common sense should tell you, you have to pay to live. Procrastination is one of the most common and deadliest diseases and its toll on success and happiness is heavy. One can never consent to creep, when one feels an impulse to soar. An idle mind is a devil's workshop. Man is happier who lives on his own labor.

In The Circles Of Life there is….

(No free lunch)

Hanging from the roof top a bug light hangs. Below the bug light there is a fly roll catcher filled with glue. Along came Sing, the lizard and noticed the insects attached to it. This was a sight to behold because he had never seen anything like this, what a lucky break. The fly catcher had been hanging there for weeks and not only did it catch flies but many more insects was stuck and died on the strip.

Sing the lizard lived on the property and knew every inch of it, he constantly roam around the deck living a care free life. He was known for always singing and wanting a free lunch. This was going to be a very easy meal for a hungry lizard a strip of dead insect seems to be a dream come. What a feast to behold, flies, ants, moths and many others. He crawled down the bug light to the area the fly strip was attached and crawled down the strip devouring the dead insects as he made his way down the strip. He was much larger and stronger than the bugs captured nothing could hold him down. Once he came to the end of the strip and had devoured all the insects he was stuffed. He tried to leap from the strip but was too heavy and too stuck.

Sing could not leap, turn nor go forward because too much glue was attached to his little legs and he was stuck. He never thought about the reason the others had not survived he thought of the feast and himself. Always look before you leap. Trying to get something for nothing can make you a free lunch.

Make your mark: We first make our habits, and then our habits make us. How much of our talents are being wasted for a care free life.

11

Wealth

o o o o o o o o o o o o o o o o o o o o o o o o o o o o o o o o o o o o o
What a man is or woman is not what he or she has, is the measure
of real wealth.

—*(Proverbs)*

Life is funny it seems the one thing that elude us is satisfaction. Some single people want to be married and some married want to be single. Some poor people
want to be rich and some rich want to be poor. Will this bring happiness or more
misery? We don't know for sure. The grass may seem greener on the other side
but it still has to be watered. There are your unique ones that want it all no matter what price they have to pay. Some because of greed rather than end a relationship equally they would rather kill than part with a car, home or the family
fortune.

I worked as a keypunch operator in my early career. Two operators would be
assigned to a remote trailer placed in a large warehouse. We worked in these
remotes processing orders for shipment. I worked with an older lady with dark
brown hair and the body of a teenager. For her age she looked a lot younger and
she was married to a man twenty years her senior. They had been married for a
long time but over the years he was becoming more controlling and jealous. One
day she did not show up or call work. No one even her kids did not know her
whereabouts. The husband claimed she had just ran off and left her valuables.
They held her position one year before assigning it to someone else. The story
now a year later was cold and forgotten, except by the ones that loved her most.
She raised Doberman Pinchers as a hobby and he was still taken care of them.
One day while visiting the stepfather the son was playing with the dog and he
notice the dog started digging in a certain spot and it was there she was discovered sixteen feet from the house buried in the yard. She never left the house.

What about those so set on getting rich they save, save, save and become so cheap until they become warp and live in poverty. Some rich people are poor and some poor people have great wealth. Being kidnapped and held for ransom never worry the poor man. Most of the rich are in constant worry of people taking their money. You can't take your money with you but you can send it ahead by helping others. It is possible to give away and become richer; it is possible to hold on too tight and lose everything. He or she who loves money shall never have enough. Be happy and enjoy yourself as long as you can. Eat, drink and enjoy the fruit of your labor because you don't know whether the person you leave the fruit of your labor to will be wise or a fool.

Many senior citizens that have scrimp and saved all of their lives just to become victims of scams and abuse. In the news recently a lady that prized herself on being thrifty and cheap, had saved over six hundred thousand dollars. She had retired and became ill, gave power of attorney to her trusted nice. Money changes people especially if they are not use to it. The niece bought her and her husband a new car. All new furniture for the home, remodeled and broke the lady bank account. Contentment isn't getting what we want but being satisfied with what we have.

My next door neighbor had a sister that had to be placed in a nursing home because her husband died and with no kids she could not maintain the upkeep of everything. She had saved for sixty years forbidding her many vacations, nice transportation and other luxuries. She gave my neighbor who was her youngest brother power of attorney and he took care of her personal needs. Due to the fact she had money and property she had to pay cash without the support of Medicare. The money that took her sixty years was all accounted for and gone in three years. You can prepare for the future but there are no guarantees even with the best of plans. What a man or woman is, not what he or she has, is the measure of real wealth.

In The Circles Of Life you will see....

(The Insatiable Greed Of Hetty Green)

Back in the late 1800's the world's richest woman was also the world's stingiest. Though she had millions in the bank, she dressed like a street hag and lived like a pauper. As a child, Hetty Robinson learned to read from the financial pages, which she would recite to her wealthy father. At age 30 she inherited one million dollars and over the course of the next 50 years, she shrewdly manipulated stocks and bonds until her fortune grew to nearly 100 million. Her financial wizardry and infamous stock manipulation title her, The Witch of Wall Street.

Although she was a genius at making money, she developed a hatred of spending it. She married Edward Green another millionaire but made him sign a prenuptial agreement not to claim any of her money. When he went broke speculating on stocks, they separated and Hetty, though she had vast wealth raised her two children under dingy conditions, moving from one cheap hotel to another to avoid paying personal property taxes. To save money on clothes and laundry soap, she wore the same dress every day and washed only the bottom portion that touched the ground. Hetty's reluctance to spend money reached horrifying proportions when her son, Ned, injured his knee. She took him to a charity ward to be treated. Unfortunately for Ned, a doctor recognized the millionaire mother and demanded payment. She refused to pay and treated the boy's injury herself.

After two years, his leg had to be amputated. She was too cheap to rent an office so she conducted her financial dealings from the bank where she kept her fortune, threatening to withdraw it if the bank officers refused to let her use an available desk. When she was feeling unhappy, she would sometimes sit on the marble floor of the bank's vault and admire her notes and securities, which she filed in the specially made pockets of her petticoat. For her meals she would warm up a bowl of oatmeal on the radiator or take out a ham sandwich, unwrapped, from one of her pockets. Hetty's lifelong stinginess even played a role in her death in 1916 at the age of 81. She suffered a stroke while arguing over the price of milk. Her son Ned hired nurses to care for her before she died, but had them dress in street clothes for fear that Hetty's condition would worsen if she realized money was being spent to pay nursing bills. As a final irony, Ned, who inherited much of his mother's fortune, became an extravagant spender. He threw his millions away on lavish parties, expensive jewelry, yachts, even diamond studded chamber pots.

Make your mark: The fact is we all have something in common that someday death, the kind old nurse will rock us all to sleep but wealth will be left behind.

12

Appreciation

o o o o o o o o o o o o o o o o o o o o o o o o o o o o o o
What you possess in the world will be found at the day of your death to belong to someone else. But what you are will be yours forever.

—*(Henry Van Dyke)*

It is not how much we have but how much we enjoy that make happiness.

When all is said and done success without happiness is the worst kind of failure. Working as a caregiver has a way of opening your eyes to how fragile life is. You can be here today and gone today.

One of my closet friends and I was talking on the phone as we so often do about our children and everything was fine. After about three weeks I had not heard from her and became concern. With persistence I was able to contact her just to learn one week after I had spoken to her she received a call from her son whom wife in her early thirties had passed away a year earlier from a blood clot of the brain. They had an infant child and he was rearing the child with the help of an aunt. He called that Monday and said he didn't feel well but he was not the type to complain. He lived out of town and she told him if he was not feeling well in a few days she was coming to see him. By that Friday he was hospitalize and moments after she arrived he was dead. He developed a virus that attacked his liver and he passed away in his early thirties. Even now she has a positive attitude.

Live full lives and die empty, give life all you got. So often we try to hold on to material things we love and thinking our love ones will too. Some will and some won't. Most of the time when one dies most of the items ends up at goodwill. One man's treasure is another man's trash. There are times they don't even take the hangers from the clothes they just reach, grab, and deliver. I've even attended estate sales that every item was up for sale, prized collections, artifacts, pictures and all kind of goodies for a little of nothing. To be alive only to material possession is to live in shallow. You can build your riches on earth unfortunately in death you have to leave it behind.

There is a movie called 'Ice' and part of the northern country fell 100 degrees below zero. Suddenly all living things began to freeze including people. One particular architect had designed this upscale beautiful home with collectable furniture from all over the world, the best literature to die for. They had to use the furniture and literature for fuel to stay alive. One couple father had dedicated millions to a hospital and received a plaque to be placed on the hospital wall. When the couple child became ill they were turned away. The couple had accumulated plenty of wealth but could not save their child life. They owned this financial institution that held the cash they accumulated it was there where they stayed to burn the money to keep warm.

What is wealth without health? Some people die from lack of food, shelter and medication when some place millions of dollars on the shelf to collect dust. Some even turn their backs on family and friends to possess it.

Animals and insects know their true purpose in life. Man has been given dominion over the earth but not control. Man is the only creature that would lose sight of his purpose and swell out of control for material gain. One man or woman life touches so many other lives, when he or she is not around it leaves a big hole. Mother Nature, such as hurricanes, tornadoes, floods, disease, and blizzard, you can't control, have killed more people than guns, murderers, and drugs, but these you can control. Don't forget the people you love on your way to the top because I have never heard anyone say on their deathbed: I wish I would have spent more time with my money and at work! Plenty of people missed their share of happiness not because they never find it, but because they didn't stop to enjoy it. What you possess in the world will be found at the day of your death to belong to someone else. But what you are will be yours forever.

In The Circle of Life you will meet....

(The Rich Man)

There was this man and he was rich in land and jewels but he wanted more. He had clothes, cars, homes but he wanted it all. Never appreciating what he had family, friends and his health. One day he heard about this town called Basset, there you could buy and own for a small price all the land you could travel by feet in a day. The man traveled to Basset to meet the land owner and was showed the most beautiful land your eyes could see. The owner said, you can have all the land you can travel in a day for a thousand dollars or that amount in rubies.

The man wanted to sleep on it and the next morning decided he would do it. Early that morning he met the land owner and gave him his price. Many of the town's people heard about it and decided they would be there to cheer the man on.

That morning he was ready, all this will be mine he thought and he began running and he walked and he ran looking and admiring the beautiful land he would own. He ran until he realized he had gone a little farther than he'd planned and quickly turned around and headed back. As he began to approach the town he could see the town's people cheering him own. He began to run faster and faster because time was running out. The louder the people cheered the faster he ran and as he reached the finish line he leaped with all the energy he had and fell dead. The people was stunned and the land owner just laughed, because many have tried to own all of the land and all of the jewels and all he needed was six feet of land from his head to his toe.

Make your mark: Sometime not appreciating what you do have, trying to get what you don't have can cause you to lose it all.

13

Action

Only began and the mind grows heated; only began and the task
will be completed.

—*(Goethe)*

For a long time I was derailed because I listen to what people said and not
watched what they did. Some people are so articulate in their conversation and
can explain any failure so beautifully you become mesmerized and not look at the
action in their life. The emotion and feeling that plays into their con is outstand-
ing. One day after valuable time has passed you realize this person is all talk and
no action. Sometime you have to let go of worn out ideas, worn out conditions
and worn out relationships.

I had the opportunity to work for Goodwill, I named it, Work will because
there was nothing there but, work. I had the opportunity to work with some
young people and a particular one stood out, he would come to work and everyone could be totally involved in getting the job done. Instead he would come in
and just talk, harass and just keep everyone from working but he associated talking, with action. Many think if they just talk about an accomplishment that is the
same as doing it. Work brings profit, talk brings poverty, it is better to get your
hands dirty and eat, than to be too proud to work and starve. If you are waiting
for good fortune to smile on you, that first social security check might arrive at
your door first. Talk without action is dead. In other words some can talk the talk
but can't walk the walk.

Determine what you want your life to be like and get into action and make it
happen. You cannot travel within and stand without because he that think by the
inch and talk by the yard should be kicked by the foot. Do not mistake activity
for achievement, busyness does not equal productiveness. The doors of opportu-

nity are marked "push and pull' you cannot win if you don't began. Don't be afraid of pressure remember that pressure is what turns a lump of coal into a diamond. If you want the rainbow, you have got to put up with the rain.

I received a call one morning from a buddy of mine, he was in his late forties and single. He asks me was I sitting down and I said yes. While having dinner with his sister and her family he had a stroke. He did not have high blood pressure and he had not been ill. The doctors had no answers. One side of his body was left paralyzed. When I visited him he assured me he would be back to work in six weeks because he could not afford to be off. I had my doubts but did not show it. He went through physical therapy and took action for his recovery. In six weeks he was back at work as good as new. I know people today that have not improved, but he had the determination to succeed, defeat was not an option. Friends and family were there with their support. Put others before yourself and you can become a leader among men because nothing stand still; everything is constantly changing whether it seem to be or not.

The principle of physics states that the entire universe is in constant motion. From fear to faith, from loneliness to love, from self doubt to self discovery, your dreams, hope and purpose mark time until you start them to marching. I am just as guilty of this as many others talking with no action such as writing this book. Sometime you have to take the first step in faith. You don't have to see the staircase, just the first step. Whatever is oftenest viewed with the inner eye reveals it secrets and hands out it gift. These stimulate the mind and give it definite direction. Lucky is what others will call you when your hard work produces results.

A word fitly spoken is like apples of gold in a setting of silver. Chose your words and action well and stand by them they will go marching down the years in the lives you touched. Only began and the mind grows heated; only began and the task will be completed.

In The Circles Of Life you can help with....

(The Mule and the Well)

A farmer who owned an old mule took this mule everyplace he went they were very close. One day the farmer had some important business to attend in town he decided to leave the mule tied up. Somehow the mule got loose and began grazing. The mule not use to being left alone began wandering about the farm. There was an old well that was left unattended and somehow the mule fell into it.

When the man arrived home and realized the mule was missing he looked everywhere for the mule but could not found him. As the man began to enter the house, he heard a sound in the well. The old man had a long rope and tried to pull the old mule out; no matter what the old man did he could not help the mule.

The man began to cry and said after assessing the situation he decided it was hopeless. The man decided if he could not pull him out of the well he could at least give him a good burial. He began to haul dirt to the well so he could put the mule of his misery. He began to shovel dirt into the well, initially the old mule was hysterical, but as the farmer continued shoveling and the dirt hit his back a thought struck him. It suddenly dawned on him to go into action every time a shovel of dirt landed on his back he should shake it off and pack the dirt under his feet. Each time he would shovel dirt the mule got higher and higher no matter how painful the blows or how distressing the situation seemed the old mule fought against panic and just kept right on SHAKING IF OFF AND STEPPING UP! It wasn't long before the old mule, battered and exhausted, stepped triumphantly out of the well.

Make your mark: Action changes things when there seems there is not hope and all else is done determination takes over.

14

Thieves

Time is the most valuable asset you have it is like money in the bank if is used wisely.

—*(John Clemont Stone)*

Since the beginning of time there have existed gangs, wars and thieves but there are different kinds of thieves. Some thieves steal your money and jewelry, some thieves steal your cars and some will steal anything that is not nailed down. But the worst kinds of thieves are those that will steal your joy and peace of mind. People that are negative, cynical and gossip all the time you better look out. Those that gossip to you will gossip about you. Get toxic people out of your life. There has never been a statue contributed to a critic. It takes a lot of energy to get where you want to go. You can run faster with a hundred people that want to go then one wrapped around you neck saying no. Surround yourself with people that will encourage and edify you. There is an old parable that says, "there is life and death in the tongue." Anyone that provokes family and friends to anger and resentment will finally have nothing and no one worthwhile left. They rob themselves of joy and peace. What you plant positive or negative you will receive. In other words what you reap, is what you sow, you can't plant apples and expect peaches.

Many people never know there greatness because they spread themselves to thin becoming sidetrack by secondary activities, never knowing how to say no even to the negative. One day you wake up behind on your dreams and your bills. I am convinced that life is ten percent of what happens to you and ninety percent of how you react to it. Some people tongue has gained them great power and they made life worth living, a new civilization. Some people tongue has gained them great power and they created a holocaust, mass destruction. The words you speak can create your future.

My girlfriend whom is single was telling me about this date she had with a wonderful guy. He took her to an exclusive restaurant and gave her expensive flowers and wonderful compliments. During the entire dinner she talked about her past lover and what a disappointment he was. Her entire conversation was negative and about the past. He listen the entire evening very attentively. After dinner he informed her he would not be seeing her anymore and she asked why not? His reply was he was looking for a lovely evening with her and she spent the evening with her old lover, the past and he was in the present. She stole his joy for the evening

Low self esteem, stress, guilt, doubt, hatred, fear and worry these are the worst kind of thieves and can cause your drive and determination to become warp. These are the kind you do not notice and they are so gradual some don't realize they are being robbed until they are left behind. People who would never think of committing suicide or ending their lives think nothing of dribbling their lives away in useless hours ever day. We may live in an imperfect world but the frontiers are not all closed and doors are not all shut. Your only limitations are those you set up in your own mind, or permit others to set up for you. You are opportunity and you must knock on the door leading to your destiny.

There are seeds of self destruction in all of us that will bear only unhappiness if allowed to grow, wake up and live. Can you pick olives from a fig tree or figs from a grape vine? No you can't draw fresh water from a salty pool. Seek what you do want in life and let go of that you don't want. The saddest summery of a life contains three descriptions: could have, might have, and should have. People have the incredible ability to major in minor things and lose valuable time. Many can tell you why you cannot succeed and why you should not even try but get rid of these thieves before they steal your dreams. It may be insane to live with a dream but it is madness to live without one. When you want to do something you have never done you must become someone you have never been.

Yesterday is a canceled check; tomorrow is a promissory note and today is cash on hand. Time is the most valuable asset you have it is like money in the bank if it is used wisely.

In The Circles Of Life look out for …

(K-Mart Shoppers)

Cathy dropped off her kids at soccer practice and drove over to K-Mart to buy toothpaste, a hairbrush, and a comb. She had just started searching for these items when an elderly woman walked up to her. "Forgive me for being so familiar," the woman said, "but you look so much like my daughter. You see, I lost her in a boating accident four month ago. You look just like her. You even move like her. Would you mind if I walk with you a little bit? I'm so lonely for her. Cathy was a kind person. "Of course," she replied, "I'd be happy to." As the two made their way through the aisles, the woman shopped and put various items in her cart. Cathy picked up the few things she was looking for.

The woman told Cathy all about her daughter and what a wonderful girl she had been. She asked Cathy about herself. Cathy told her she was a schoolteacher and showed her pictures of her family. When they had finished their shopping, the woman entered the checkout line ahead of Cathy. As her purchases were being rung up, the woman turned to Cathy and said, "You know, I never got to say goodbye to my daughter. That hurts me so much, would you mind terribly just stepping back and saying, 'Goodbye, Mama; and giving me a big hug?" Cathy found that rather strange, but the whole visit with the woman had been a little strange. "Yes, of course," she said. "I'll be happy to do that." Cathy stepped back, put out her arms and said "Goodbye, Mama." Then she moved forward and gave the woman a big hug. "Oh, thanks you so much, my dear," said the woman. "You're so kind.

Cathy was a little flustered as she glanced around at the people in line behind her. She turned back to see the woman pushing her cart out the door. Cathy moved to the cash register and put her toothpaste, hairbrush and comb on the conveyor belt. The checkout clerk scanned them into the register. "That'll be 357.49," the clerk said. "No, no," said Cathy. "There must be some mistake. I just have these few things." "Yes," said the cashier, "but your mother told me to put the TV on your bill."

Make your mark: Sometimes things are not what they seem, be careful of thieves, some take kindness as a sign of weakness.

15

Vanity

o o o o o o o o o o o o o o o o o o o o o o o o o o o o o o o o o o o o
Beauty is only skin deep.

—*(The Temptation)*

Some of us somehow manage to take it to a higher level. Models, actors and actresses, sportsman and politicians fame makes this the fashion of today. Everybody wants to be beautiful. Some goes as far as to be under the knife two and three times a year, tummy tuck, nose job, breast implants, you name it there is no reason to be ugly today. James Brown, teeth implants, Dolly Parton, body tucks, Michael Jackson, nose job was done to improve their looks. Anything can be changed about your body today if you are ready to risk it.

We have come a long way since the day of Dr. Frankenstein, he was scorned for taking body parts and trying to create life with them. History has a way of changing things it is possible the work he did then may have given us the progress we have today. It is better to look into a person heart than at their face. Many are judge by how thy look than who they are. Some people that are overweight in our since of weight speak of the horrible things people say to them and how mean they are treated at times.

Hope and change of attitude is the companion of power and mother of success; for whoso hopes strongly has within him or her gifts of miracles. It is said ten men banded together in love can do what ten thousand separately would fail in. Living in Atlanta I met many people, this one particular lady and I became close and she weighed at least three hundred pounds at the time we were hanging out. It wasn't because she ate a lot it was because of her thyroids. She was very active in basketball, dancing and working two full time jobs. We would even dress a like can you imagine at the time I was about ninety five pounds. She would have some of the most beautiful clothes designed for her.

At this time stomach by pass was fairly new and she had it done. She lost a lot of weight and almost her life. This surgery is not for everyone they had to undo what was done and she is healthy and heavy today but alive and happy. Vanity can be an advantage and a disadvantage if is not used properly. Electricity is good to turn on lights and to use household appliances but if you misbehave and grab hold of a bare wire of electricity it can kill you, just as fire is good for cooking, but if you sit in the middle of a fire you will get burned. Necessary surgeries are good and have improved many lives but do your research without proper information and physician many have been maimed.

We are all extremely valuable, worthwhile significant individuals even though some present circumstances may have you feeling otherwise, release your brakes and stop holding back. Learn to love yourself and those that love you, because unconditional love has no price. More than any other human problem, loneliness, the absence of meaningful human connection, drains the joy and sense of purpose from our lives.

My adopted cousin was burned in a fire that disfigured her face, and burned most of her fingers to nubs. Her body somewhat disfigured. Although there were many obstacles to get her into public school my aunt did. Since she was raised in the community she was accepted without prejudice. After you come to love and accept someone you don't see their faults or looks but what is in their heart. We must combine the toughness of the serpent and the softness of the dove, a tough mind and a tender heart.

Author Alexander Penny once asked hundred of males to define the word sexy. The seven most responses were: Self confident, composed, intelligent, self assured, friendly, feminine, and at ease with their body. Beauty and having a voluptuous body were way down on the list, and nobody said they wanted a woman that looked like a fashion model. Beauty is only skin deep.

In The Circles Of Life you will meet …

(The Three Spinsters)

There was once a girl who was lazy and would not spin and her mother could not persuade her to do what she would. At last the mother became angry and out of patience gave her a good beating and she cried out, loudly. At that moment the Queen was going by; As she heard the crying she stopped; going into the house she asked the mother, "why was she beating her daughter so everyone in the street could hear her cries?' The woman was ashamed to tell her daughter's laziness, so she said, "I cannot stop her from spinning; she is for ever at it and I am poor and cannot furnish her with flax enough.' Then the Queen answered, 'I like nothing better than the sound of the spinning wheel, and always feel happy when I hear it humming; let me take your daughter with me to the castle I have plenty of flax, she shall spin there to her heart's content.' The mother was only too glad of the offer and the Queen took the girl with her.

When they reached the castle the Queen showed her three rooms which were filled with the finest flax as full as they could hold. "Now you can spin me this flax," she said, "and when you can show it me all done you shall have my eldest son for a bridegroom; you may be poor, but I make nothing of, that your industry is dowry enough," The girl was inwardly terrified, for she could not have spun the flax, even if she were to live to be a hundred years old and were to sit spinning every day of her life from morning to evening. And when she found herself alone she began to weep, and sat for three days without putting her hand to it. On the third day the Queen came and when she saw that nothing had been done of the spinning she was surprised; but the girl excused herself by saying that she had not been able to begin because of the distress she was in at leaving her home and her mother. The excuse contented the Queen, who said; however, as she went away, "tomorrow you must begin to work." When the girl found herself alone again she could not tell how to help herself or what to do, and in her perplexity she went and gazed out of the window.

There she saw three women passing by, and the first of them had a broad flat foot, the second had a big under-lip that hung down over her chin, and the third had a remarkably broad thumb. Then all of them stopped in front of the window and called out to know what it was the girl wanted. She told them all her need, and they promised her their help, and said, "Then will you invite us to your wedding, and not be ashamed of us, and call us your cousins, and let us sit at the table; if you will promise this, we will finish off your flax spinning in a very short time. "With my heart, answered the girl; only come in now, and began at once." Then these same women came in and she cleared a space in the first room for them to sit and carry on their spinning. The first on drew out the thread and moved the treadle that turned the wheel, the second moistened the thread, the third twisted it and rapped with her finger on the table and as often as she rapped a heap of yarn fell to the ground, and it was most beautifully spun. But the girl hid the three spinsters out of the Queen's sight, and only showed her as often as she came, the heaps of well spun yarn; and there was no end to the praises she received. When the first room was empty they went on to the second and then the third, so that at last it was finished. Then the three women took their leave, saying to the girl, "Do not forget what you have promised, and it will be all the better for you. So when the girl took the Queen and showed her the empty rooms, and the great heaps of yarn, the wedding was at once arranged, and the bridegroom rejoiced that he should have so clever and diligent a wife and praised her exceedingly.

I have three cousins," said the girl," and as they have shown me a great deal of kindness, I would not wish to forget them in my good fortune; may I be allowed to invite them to the wedding, and to ask them to sit at the table with us? The Queen and the bridegroom said at once, "There is no reason against it. So when the feast began in came the three spinsters strange guise, and the bride said "Dear cousins, you are welcome." Oh," said the bridegroom, "how come you have such dreadfully ugly relations?" And then he went up to the first spinster and said how is it that you have such broad flat foot? With treading, answered she, with treading." Then he went up to the second and said, how is it that you have such great hanging lips? With licking," answered she, with licking." Then he asked the third, how is it that you have such a broad thumb?" With twisting thread," answered she, with twisting thread. Then the bridegroom said that from that time forward his beautiful bride should never touch a spinning wheel and she escaped that tiresome life of flax spinning.

Make your mark: The great thing in life is not what people can do for you but what you can do for people, because beauty is in the eyes of the beholder.

16

Jealousy

○ ○
The worst prison is a closed heart.

—(Pope John Paul 11)

Have you fifty friends? It is not enough, have you one enemy? It is too much, it is impossible not to attract individuals who would rejoice in your downfall. Man is born to survive, although his end is inevitable. As your success grows you will soon discover that there are others who would delight in pulling you down from your perch.

It is the mind that make good or ill, that make wrath or happy, rich or poor. Negative thoughts can lead to envy, resentment, jealousy then destruction. People are like tea bags: They never realize their strength until they are dropped in hot water. It takes a clever man to turn cynic and a wise man to be clever enough not to. It is not because things are difficult that we do not dare, it is because we do not dare that they are difficult.

From dream to nightmare is the headline about Jack Whittaker the power ball jackpot winner of 314.9 million. In his darkest moments wondered if winning was really worth it. His wife divorced him when in fact they once went to church each Sunday together. His drug addict grandmother died. With all his money he could not cure his daughter of Cancer. He endures constant requests for money with lots of sad stories. He has no friends as before, some became jealous and resentful. Jack Whittaker was already a self made millionaire but by the sweat of his brow. People feel he did not earn this so he should give it away. People respect what you earn but not what you are given.

You may get burned, but you don't have to be bitter. Bitterness is like taking poison and expects your enemy to die. A relaxed attitude lengthens a man's life, jealousy rots it away, and it is more dangerous than anger. It is better to eat soup with someone you love, then to eat steak with someone you hate. Compliment people, build castles don't dig graves. You teach your mind to drive a car, type one hundred words a minute, play a piano, then once learned place your mind on auto pilot. This can be for good habits or for bad habits, discard negative thoughts.

You can add youth to your life by staying flexible, adaptable and open minded. Do not permit your mental arteries to harden. Wherever there is jealousy or selfishness there will be disorder and no harmony. The fountain of youth is within you. One of my closet friends now in her seventies and single still date, drive, work, and travel, she lives her life to the fullest. You do not grow old; you become old by not growing. Sometime we have to close our eyes to the faults of others and open them to our own.

Failure to communicate has caused grief to my dear friend today for the love of his son and grandsons, but refuse to initiate any action. He hasn't seen his son in years and he has never seen or hugged his grandsons. He is now an old man but still hasn't even tried to see his grandsons due to hardening of the arteries in his thinking. His son married and did not invite him to the wedding; somehow they lost each other alone the way. Now by letting this persist it is out of control and nobody is winning especially the grandchildren. The greatest use of life is to spend it on something that will make a difference. Learn to listen from within because one of the most tragic things about human is that we have a tendency to put off living. Our main business is not to see what lies dimly at a distance, but to do what lies clearly at hand. Negative thinking and fear can kill hopes and dreams. The worst prison is a closed heart.

In The Circles Of Life just look out....

(The Window)

There were two men, both seriously ill, who occupied the same small hospital room. One man was allowed to sit up in his bed for an hour each afternoon to help drain the fluid from his lungs. His bed was next to the room's only window. The other man had to spend all his time flat on his back. The men talked for hours on end. They spoke of their wives and families, their homes, their jobs, their involvement in the military service, where they had been on vacation. And every afternoon when the man in the bed by the window could sit up, he would pass the time by describing to his roommate all the things he could see outside the window. The man in the other bed began to live for those one hour period where his world would be broadened and enlighten by all the activity and color of the outside world.

The window overlooked a park with a lovely lake, the man said. Ducks and swans played on the water while children sailed their model boats. Lovers walked arm amid flowers of every color of the rainbow. Grand old trees graced the landscape, and a fine view of the city skyline could be seen in the distance. As the man by the window described all this in exquisite detail, the man on the other side of the room would close his eyes and imagine the picturesque scene. One warm afternoon the man by the window described a parade passing by. Although the other man couldn't hear the band, he could see it in his mind's eye as the gentleman by the window portrayed it with descriptive words. Unexpectedly, an alien thought entered his head, why should he have all the pleasure of seeing everything while I never get to see anything? It isn't fair.

As the thought fermented the man felt ashamed at first. But as the days passed and he missed seeing more sights, his envy eroded into resentment and soon turned him sour. He began to brood and he found himself unable to sleep. He should be by the window, that thought now controlled his life. Late one night as he lay staring at the ceiling, the man by the window began to cough. He was choking on the fluid in his lungs. The other man watched in the dimly lit room as the struggling man by the window groped for the button to call for help. The man due to his sour mind did not say a word and the man died.

The next morning the nurse found him and was bewildered because he never pressed the button for help. Once he was removed she stripped his bed. The man that observed him asks the nurse could he be placed by the window and she said yes. Once by the window the man struggled to sit up and enjoy the scenery when he looked out the window all he saw was a brick wall. He watched him die so he could see nothing.

Make your mark: Negative thoughts can turn to envy resentment and eventually poison your mind.

17

Arrogance

o o o o o o o o o o o o o o o o o o o o o o o o o o o o o o o o o o
As a man thinks so is he

—(James Allen)

Many times you here do as I say but not as I do. Some can dish it out but can take it. Some parents are truly guilty of this. Children watch more of what you do than what you say. For instance you tell them not to lie. You get a visitor you don't want to see and you tell them to say you are not at home when in fact you are hiding in the bathroom. Maybe you get a phone call tell them I just left for the store when in fact you just returned. You become angry and insist that they get an education when in fact you always slipped out the schools back door and played hooky never to receive a diploma. You make them go to church but you stay home and watch the game. Thinking their going will somehow help you get in the pearly gates. You insist that they show you respect when every word out your mouth is profanity.

I got in trouble once for repeating what my grandmother said. One day an insurance man came to the house to collect on her policy, in earlier years they came to your home. This particular day she told me to tell him she was not at home. When he asked for my grandmother I said, she said, she is not at home. The word she, got me in trouble, I should have said she is not at home. What did I know I was just a kid? Be careful what you say and how you say it because it could come back to bite or spank you.

Our lives are like mirrors people see the reflections of your true actions. I was having a conversation with a man that was living with friends and was not compensating them for his stay. He had an eloquent conversation but he was not keeping up his end of the bargain. During the conversation he was telling me he'd talked to his grown son that was living at home with his mother. He told his son he needed to be more responsible and each time he was paid to compensate her for his needs. He told me how he had reprimanded him for not being a man. I was listening to this and I asked him, how can you reprimand him when you yourself is living under the roof of another man and not compensating him? Two men just as two women cannot run a household. Someone has to take charge and to me that would be the ones paying the bills. How can you tell your son how to be a man when if fact you are not showing him how? This guy was beside himself he did not expect that kind of question and he had no answer. He never thought about his actions. That next week the man left without any good bys. People do watch what you do and not what you say because action speaks louder than words. As a man thinks so is he.

In The Circles Of Life you will meet....

(The Father and His Daughter)

A little girl was given so many picture books on her seventh birthday that her father, who should have run his office and let her mother run the home, thought his daughter should give one or two of her new books to a little neighbor boy named Robert, who had dropped in, more by design than by chance. now, taking books, or anything else, from a little girl is like taking arms from an Arab, or candy from a baby, but the father of the little girl had his way and Robert got two of her books." "After all, that leaves you with nine," said the father, who thought he was a philosopher and a child psychologist, and couldn't shut his big famous mouth on the subject.

A few weeks later, the father went to his library to look up "father" in the Oxford English Dictionary, to fest his eyes on the praise of fatherhood through the centuries, but he couldn't find volume F-G, and then he discovered that three others were missing, too A-B, L-M, and V-Z. He began a probe of his household, and soon learned what become of the four missing volumes. "A man came to the door this morning," said his little daughter," "and he didn't know how to get from here to Torrington, or from Torrington to Winsted, and he was a nice man, much nicer than Robert, and so I gave him four of your books. After all, there are thirteen volumes in the Oxford English Dictionary, and that leaves you nine.

Mark your mark: What is good for the goose is also good for the gander.

18

Pride

One hundred years from now it will not matter what kind of car I drove, what kind of house I lived in, or how much money I had in the bank, but the world may be a better place because I made a difference in a person's life. We should seize every opportunity to give encouragement. Encouragement is oxygen to the soul.

Some people are committing suicide because they cannot live up to others expectation especially in young teens today. My dad wants me to play football, and I love art, my wife wants me to be the Chief Executive Officer in charge of everyone and I just want to do sales, my friends want me to try their new businesses and all I want is to enjoy their company, my church wants me to usher, sing, and help with the youth but I just want to teach Sunday school. These demands can cause discomfort from trying to spread yourself too thin. It is good to remember that the tea kettle, although up to its neck in hot water, continues to sing. There are cantankerous sorts who disagree merely to start an argument. The fastest runners and greatest heroes don't always win races and battles and wisdom, intelligence and skills don't always make you healthy, rich or popular. We each have our share of bad luck.

I was sitting with a client an elderly lady who had plenty of wealth but very bad health. A matter of fact she was knocking on death's door. One day her son came over and brought her a beautiful plant and thought she would be pleased. Instead of appreciating the plant she started complaining about a lamp she wanted to be replaced. I was disappointed because she was not expressing to her children and grandchildren her love and affection. She was completely blinded by material gain. Many use their money as a form of manipulation instead of appreciation that they miss out on the true blessings in life. A few days later the old lady fell and broke her hip as so many do. She had wealth but do to fear of spending she chose a rehabilitation facility that was free the first ninety days. She could afford the best of care around the clock. I pleaded with her to reconsider, because you get what you pay for and you can imagine what you get when it is free, poor treatment. Working with her I noticed she had spent so much energy keeping people away to protect her assets even her children that in the end she was very much alone.

One day while visiting her I ask if she could do something different in her life what would it be and she said I would spend more time with people. Within two weeks the lady had bed soars, due to lack of attention. They didn't know, nor care about her money, cars, and huge mansion she resided. She was use to giving orders and controlling others lives, now someone was controlling hers. Someday you do have to give it up, ready or not. One day while visiting, I could see the fear in her eyes. She had called for a bed pan and was left on it for one hour when I arrived, pressed against her skin and bones. When something sound to good to be true and you can afford what you know is true, think about it. Within three week her health deteriorated and she died. She didn't even get her free ninety days.

You can't please everybody and everybody is not going to try to please you. Do not let others or material gain make you turn your back on those you love because you can be here today and gone today and everything you have gained including life will be gone. You can please some of the people some of the time but not all the people all of the time.

In The Circles Of Life you will meet....

(The Father, Son and the Donkey)

One day a father and his son were driving their donkey to market. They had not gone far when some girls saw them and broke out laughing. "Look!" cried one, "Look at those fools! How silly they are to be trudging on foot when the donkey might be carrying one of them on his back." This seemed to make sense, so the father lifted his son on the donkey and walked along contentedly by his side. They trod on for a while until they met some women who spoke to the son scornfully. "You should be ashamed of yourself, you lazy rascal. What do you mean by riding when you poor old father has to walk? It shows that no one respects age any more. The least you can do is get down and let your father rest his old bones." Red with shame, the son dismounted and made his father get on the donkey's back.

They had gone only a little further when they met a group of young fellows who mocked them. "What cruel old man!" jeered one of the fellows? "There he sits, selfish an comfortable, while the poor boy has to stumble along the dusty road to keep up with him." So the father lifted the son up, and the two of them rode along. However, before they reached the market place, a townsman stopped them. "Have you no feeling for dumb creatures?" he shouted. "The way you load that little animal is a crime. You two men are better able to carry the poor little beast than he you!" Wanting to do the right thing, the father and his son got off the donkey, tied his legs together, slung him on a pole, and carried him on their shoulders.

When the crowd saw this spectacle the people laughed so loudly that the donkey was frightened, kicked through the cords that bound him and, falling off the pole, fell into the river and was drowned.

Make your mark: When you try to please everybody, nobody wins

19

Gossip

A wise old owl sat upon an oak; the more he saw the less he spoke; the less he spoke the more he heard; why aren't we like that wise old bird?

—*(Edward Hersey)*

Although the tongue weigh very little only a few people are able to hold it. Never say anything to hurt anyone. Sometime we have to refrain from double talk, from shrewd and canny remarks that are designed to advance our interests at someone's disadvantage. We are to turn our backs upon evil and in every way possible, do well, help people and bring blessings into their lives. In the end most aggressors always destroy themselves. People may gossip and talk about you but don't be sad, don't be angry, if life deceives you accept your grief and know this too shall pass and your time for joy will come. Anger dwells only in the bosom of fools. For every sixty seconds of anger you lose one minute of happiness.

Anything facing us is not as important as our attitude toward it, for that determines our success or failure. My hobby is fishing I can do this hours on end it is the best form or relaxation I can imagine. But it has occurred to me a fish wouldn't get caught if it would keep it mouth shut. Some people do not know when to shut up. Lives have been lost because of this, many falsely imprisoned, and some even had mental breakdowns due to underserved verbal ridicule. Relationships have been destroyed because of rumors. One night my cousins and I were out for a night of partying and two men were arguing at the bar. One of the guys was from a family that was known to be trouble; he was a member of a large clan. I don't know exactly what happened because everything happened so fast. One of the family members of the clan entered the club and was killed instantly by the man arguing at the bar because he feared this guy would help the other.

The only problem, this was one of the nice and humble members of the family that never caused any problems. He died because of fear of rumors. Man has trained, and can even tame some animals, birds, reptiles and fish, but no human being can tame the tongue.

Telling lies about someone is as harmful as hitting him or her with an axe, or wounding them with a sword, and shooting them with a sharp arrow. To hate is to be a liar, but to slander is to be a fool. Don't tell your secrets to a gossip unless you want them to broadcast it to the world.

The unspoken word never does any harm. A pessimist sees the difficulty in every opportunity; an optimist sees the opportunity in ever difficulty. Your reputation can be damage by the opinions of others, but only you yourself can damage your character. People demand freedom of speech as a compensation for the freedom of thought which they seldom use. In the transfer from mind to mouth many a fools are born but those same thoughts spring forth as a beautiful fountain when they flow through the heart. Assuming that just because you can hear, you can listen, is like assuming that just because you can see, you can read.

A wise old owl sat upon an oak; the more he saw the less he spoke; the less he spoke the more he heard; why aren't we like that wise old bird.

In The Circle Of Life you will hear …

(The Talking Skull)

There was once a man who was walking in search of food. He came upon a whitened skull lying on the ground in the hot sunlight. He approached the skull and wondered out loud, "what brought you here?" The skull's jaw began to creak and move. The curious man moved closer to the skull and heard it say,

> Woe is me, Misery!
> I cannot shed a tear.
> Woe is me, Misery!
> My mouth has bought me here.

The man was amazed! "A talking skull!" he exclaimed. He almost forgot his hunger for a moment. He was curious and asked. "How could your mouth bring you here?" Then the skull spoke again and said, "I will show you. First walk a distance in the direction my nose points and you will find some calabashes filled with grain to eat." The man walked and walked and came to some calabashes filled with grain. He was so happy to find food. He ran back to the skull and said, "Thank you! If I had not found these calabashes, I too might be a skeleton soon!" The skull replied, "Do not tell anyone about me or you will be sorry."

The man ran to the village. He showed the food. Everyone was glad to see the grain. The king demanded that the man come to his hut. "Where did you find this food?" he asked. Forgetting the warning of the skull, the man said, "A talking skull told me where to find the calabashes filled with grain." You are lying," said the king. "Perhaps you have stolen this food. There cannot be a talking skull." "I will take you to it, "boasted the man. "Then you will see that what I say is true." "If you are lying we will cut off your head," said the king.

The man led the king and several warriors to the place where he had seen the skull. "There it is," he said. The skull's eye socket stared like small caves. Its jaw hung open. The man leaned close to the skull and said, "Now tell everyone where to find the food." The skull sat white and silent in the Sun. "Please," said the man, a bit nervous under the glare of the king's eye,"tell everyone what you told me!" But the skull sat like a hard dry stone. The man threw himself on the ground and begged, "Show them I am not a liar! Tell them! Where is the food?" But the only sounds they heard were birds and insects. The king was outraged and commanded, "kill him. Cut off his head, for he has lied. And they cut off the man's head and left him there. In time two whitened skulls were lying next to each other on the ground in the hot sun. The first skull turned to the second and finally said,

> Woe is me! Misery!
> What I said is true.
> It was my mouth that brought me here, my friend.
> Your mouth has brought you too!

Make your mark: Be careful when you speak the life you save may be your own

20

Love

o o o o o o o o o o o o o o o o o o o o o o o o o o o o o o o o o o o o
It's a thin line between love and hate.

—(Proverbs)

Too many times we place conditions on our love. If you want to found out how strong a love is just get sick or go broke. Love is the dynamic motivation behind every worthy purpose; it is the upward thrust that lifts men to the heights. Love is the perfect antidote that floods the mind to wash away hatred, jealousy, resentment, anxiety and fear. It is tenderness and compassion, forgiveness and tolerance.

Many people have been abandoned because they were in a bad accident, lost their job, lost their sight, had a breakdown, diagnosed with a disease, or just grew old. Sometime people will abandon you when the times are tough but will return when they get better these are fair weather friends. They only come around when the weather is good but don't let it rain you will not see them. My girlfriend and her husband learned this when they decided to stop drinking and partying. Their list of friends slowly dwindle to only a handful when normally the house was a constant social event.

Even the elderly are sometime abandoned not because they can't think but because they can't keep up. Isn't it ironic when love is based on the ability to keep up? Keep up with the neighbors new cars, keep up with the overprices home association fees, keep up with the expensive clothes, keep up with the credit cards, keep up your children lifestyle, just keep it up and see what happens when you can't keep it up. Will they still love you unconditionally? During my time in the Army Reserve we would often play war games and there would be casualties. These casualties were only on paper.

I was working one day in the tag line and this young girl with a two year old son came to my desk. She was so excited about going to war and represent her country she was only about twenty one. She was so young she didn't realize the one thing war offer is tragedy and hope you don't become one of them. Some are maimed for life, minds destroys, bodies disfigured, homes and family separated.

During a tour at Fort Stewart, I met a civilian lady working in the office I was assigned. She had recently returned to her family after being separated for a while. Her husband a military sergeant continued to care for the children because he was financially able and loved them. I met her husband during this time and he was a devoted husband and loving father. She informed me she left him because of his weight. He had gained over fifty pound since their marriage. They were even childhood sweethearts married many years. He gained fifty pounds and her love and desire for him stopped. She liked him small and could not change because she was not sexually attracted to him. After a year or more of separation he met a lady that accepted him the way he was and they fell in love. She heard about this and decided she would return and try again maybe jealousy or vanity. Although she returned her love never did. It wasn't long before she left, divorced and married a smaller man she met on the base. Unconditional love, can it withstand the test of time? It's a thin line between love and hate.

(Going Home)

A story is told about a soldier who was going home after having fought in Vietnam. He called his parents from San Francisco. "Mom and Dad, I'm coming home, but I've a favor to ask. I have a friend I'd like to bring home with me. "Sure," they replied, "we'd love to meet him."

There's something you should know," the son continued. "He was hurt pretty badly in the fighting. He stepped on a land mind and lost an arm and a leg. He has nowhere else to go, and I want him to come live with us. "I'm sorry to hear that, son. Maybe we can help him find somewhere to live." "No, Mom and Dad, I want him to live with us." "Son, said the father, "You don't know what you're asking. Someone with such a handicap would be a terrible burden on us. We have our own lives to live, and we can't let something like this interfere with our lives. I think you should just come home and forget about this guy. He'll find a way to live on his own." At that point, the son hung up the phone.

The parents heard nothing more from him. A few days later, however, they received a call from the San Francisco police. Their son had died after falling from a building, they were told. The police believed it was suicide. The grief stricken parents flew to San Francisco and was taken to the city morgue to identify the body of their son. They recognized him, but to their horror they also discovered something they didn't know their son had only one arm and one leg.

Make your mark: Nothing takes the place of unconditional love.

21

Attention

"Calm, calm me more, nor let me die, before I have begun to live."

—*(Matthew Arnold)*

Some people are so busy designing a life that they forget to live. I heard once about this man that was so determine to work all the time. He would leave home early in the mornings and return after midnight. He wanted to give his family the best. For many years he would always leave the checks and money on the table.

One day he noticed the checks were piling up. The man was so busy working he never noticed the kids had grew up and left home, even the wife was gone. Life had passed him by and he never saw it coming because he had tunnel vision, he saw only what he wanted to see. This happened to a friend of mines, he never took his family on vacation, or attended school function or games with his son because he had to work, his excuse was somebody had to make a living even though his wife worked and helped with the responsibilities. He attributed it to that is the way he was raised a hundred years ago and it didn't hurt him. But it did, he ended up losing his family early in the game of life. His son was very young when the marriage ended. Sometimes it is not the money or the material things they want it is your time, a picnic, a fishing trip, a walk on the beach or just a midnight stroll. Memory is something you create for others.

"If you make your children happy now, you will make them happy twenty years from now by memory of it. Memory is the only paradise from which we cannot be driven, it keeps the past alive; and a good past is a bundle of todays well lived. Each day is a lifetime in miniature. To awaken each morning is to be born again, to fall asleep at night is to die to the day. Stop and smell the roses, see the stars and see what nature has to offer you. My love is fishing just to be among Mother Nature is a delight.

When we fail and fall short, let us forgive ourselves. Emerson wrote: Finish every day and be done with it. You have done what you could; some blunders and absurdities have crept in; forget them as soon as you can. Tomorrow is a new day; you will begin it well and serenely and with too high a spirit to be cumbered by your old nonsense." Calm, calm me more, nor let me die, before I have begun to live.

Make your mark: Take time to live. Live today as if it was your last because it could be.

In The Circles Of Life look out for....

(The Brick)

A young and very successful executive was traveling down a neighborhood street. He was going a bit too fast in his new Jaguar. He was watching for kids darting out from between parked cars and slowed down when he thought he saw something. As his car passed and no children appeared, instead, a brick smashed into the Jag's side door! He slammed on the brakes, spun the Jag back to the spot from where the brick had been thrown.

He jumped out of the car, grabbed some kid and pushed him up against a parked car, shouting, "What was that all about and who are you? Just what the heck are you doing?' Building up a head of steam, he went on. "That's a new car and that brick you threw is gonna cost you a lot of money. Why did you do it? "Please, mister, please, I'm sorry! I didn't know what else to do!" pleaded the youngster. "I threw the brick because no one else would stop." Tears were dripping down the boy's chin as he pointed around the parked car. It's my brother," he said. "He rolled off the curb and fell out of his wheelchair and I can't lift him up."

Sobbing, the boy asked the executive, "Would you please help me get him back into his wheelchair? He's hurt and he's too heavy for me. "Moved beyond words, the driver tried desperately to swallow the rapidly swelling lump in his throat. He helped the boy back into the wheelchair and took out his handkerchief and wiped the scrapes and cuts, checking to see that everything was going to be okay. "Thank you, sir! God bless you!" He then watched the boy push his brother down the sidewalk toward their home. It was a long walk back to his Jaguar, and he never did repair the side door. He kept the dent to remind him not to go through life so fast that someone would have to throw a brick at him to get his attention. Life whispers in our souls and speaks to our hearts. Sometimes, when we don't have time to listen, life throws a brick at your head.

Make your mark: Sometimes we are moving so fast we can't see the forest for the trees

Sources of Information

1.	Og Mandino	The University Of Success
2.	God Little Instruction Book For Women	Honor Books
3.	A Hero in Every Heart	H. Jackson Brown Jr.
4.	The Art Of Living Treasure Chest	Wilfred A. Peterson
5.	Spiders in The Hairdo	David Holt and Bill Mooney
6.	The Psychology of Mental Disorders	Not listed
7.	The Dynamic Laws Of Prosperity	Catherine Ponder
8.	Grimm's fairy tales	Not Listed
9.	The Inspiration Place of Daily Living	The Internet
10.	The Living Bible	King James Version
11.	Kenneth Mc Farland	
12.	G.W. Target	
13.	Harriet Beecher Stowe	
14.	Martin Luther King, Jr	
15.	Heather Forest	
16.	James Allen	
17.	Ralph Waldo Emerson	
18.	Goethe	
19.	Shakespeare	
20.	Les Brown	
21.	Dr. Allen Fromme	
22.	Booker T. Washington	
23.	Frederick Van Lessselear Day	

24.   Henry Van Dykes

25.   John Clement Stone

26.   Norman Vincent Peal

27.   The Temptation

28.   Pope John Paul II

29.   Edmond Hersey

30.   Matthew Arnold

31.   Michelle Singletary

978-0-595-47899-6
0-595-47899-9